Teacher

by JoAnn Early Macken
Photographs by Gregg Andersen

Reading consultant: Susan Nations, M.Ed., author/literacy coach/consultant

WEEKLY READER®
PUBLISHING

Please visit our web site at: www.garethstevens.com
For a free color catalog describing our list of high-quality books,
call 1-800-542-2595 (USA) or 1-800-387-3178 (Canada).
Our fax: 877-542-2596

Library of Congress Cataloging-in-Publication Data

Macken, JoAnn Early, 1953-
    Teacher / by JoAnn Early Macken.
      p. cm. — (People in my community)
    Summary: Photographs and simple text introduce the work of the teacher, who helps children
learn how to read, write, and count.
    Includes bibliographical references and index.
    ISBN-13: 978-0-8368-3593-9   ISBN-10: 0-8368-3593-X (lib. bdg.)
    ISBN-13: 978-0-8368-3600-4   ISBN-10: 0-8368-3600-6 (softcover)
    1. Teachers—Juvenile literature.   2. Teaching—Vocational guidance—Juvenile literature.
[1. Teachers. 2. Occupations.] I. Title. II. Series.
LB1775.M4222   2003
371.1—dc21   2002032964

First published in 2003 by
Weekly Reader® Books
An Imprint of Gareth Stevens Publishing
1 Reader's Digest Rd.
Pleasantville, NY 10570-7000 USA

Art direction: Tammy Gruenewald
Page layout: Katherine A. Goedheer
Photographer: Gregg Andersen
Editorial assistant: Diane Laska-Swanke

Printed in the United States of America

3 4 5 6 7 8 9 10 10 09 08

Note to Educators and Parents

Reading is such an exciting adventure for young children! They are beginning to integrate their oral language skills with written language. To encourage children along the path to early literacy, books must be colorful, engaging, and interesting; they should invite the young reader to explore both the print and the pictures.

People in My Community is a new series designed to help children read about the world around them. In each book young readers will learn interesting facts about some familiar community helpers.

Each book is specially designed to support the young reader in the reading process. The familiar topics are appealing to young children and invite them to read — and re-read — again and again. The full-color photographs and enhanced text further support the student during the reading process.

In addition to serving as wonderful picture books in schools, libraries, homes, and other places where children learn to love reading, these books are specifically intended to be read within an instructional guided reading group. This small group setting allows beginning readers to work with a fluent adult model as they make meaning from the text. After children develop fluency with the text and content, the book can be read independently. Children and adults alike will find these books supportive, engaging, and fun!

— Susan Nations, M.Ed., author, literacy coach,
and consultant in literacy development

The teacher helps children learn in school. Children learn about reading, writing, and math.

Children all around
the world go to school
to learn from their
teachers.

The teacher reads books with the students. The teacher might use a **computer** to help students learn.

computer

Teachers answer questions. Teachers also ask students questions. If you know the answer, raise your hand.

Some teachers teach many subjects, like math, reading, and writing. Some teachers teach just one subject, like art, science, or music.

13

Sometimes a teacher takes children on a field trip. They might visit a zoo or a museum. Field trips help children learn more about their subjects.

Teachers work at school and at home. At home, they correct papers and tests. They plan what to teach.

Teachers meet with adults to tell them how much their children are learning.

It's fun to share what you know.

Glossary

field trip — a visit made by a teacher and students to learn by seeing something

museum — a place to see objects of interest and value

subjects — areas of learning, such as art, math, or science

For More Information

Fiction Books

Henkes, Kevin. *Lilly's Purple Plastic Purse.*
  New York: Greenwillow Books, 1996.

Nonfiction Books

Deedrick, Tami. *Teachers.*
  Mankato, Minn.: Bridgestone Books, 1998.
Hayward, Linda. *A Day in the Life of a Teacher.*
  New York: Dorling Kindersley, 2001.
Liebman, Daniel. *I Want to Be a Teacher.*
  Willowdale, Ont.: Firefly Books, 2001.
Maynard, Christopher. *Jobs People Do.*
  New York: DK Publishing, 2001.

Web Site
Bureau of Labor Statistics Career Information
http://stats.bls.gov/k12/html/red_002.htm
What teachers do, how they prepare for the job, more
information about teaching

Index

About the Author

JoAnn Early Macken is the author of children's poetry, two rhyming picture books, *Cats on Judy* and *Sing-Along Song,* and various other nonfiction series. She teaches children to write poetry and received the Barbara Juster Esbensen 2000 Poetry Teaching Award. JoAnn is a graduate of the MFA in Writing for Children Program at Vermont College. She lives in Wisconsin with her husband and their two sons.